allergic

Megan Wagner Lloyd
and Michelle Mee Nutter

graphix
An Imprint of
SCHOLASTIC

For Lucy
M. W. L.

For Ethan
M. M. N.

This edition published by Scholastic Australia.

ISBN 978-1-76112-852-3

10 9 8 26 27 28 29

Printed in China by Hang Tai Printing Company Limited

Color flatting by Veda Kasireddy and Madison Coyne

Edited by Cassandra Pelham Fulton
Creative Director: Phil Falco
Publisher: David Saylor

Chapter One

IT WAS MY TENTH BIRTHDAY.
AND IT WAS GOING TO BE THE
BEST BIRTHDAY OF MY WHOLE LIFE.
FOR SALE
CALL MAYA

THE BEST **DAY** OF MY ENTIRE LIFE, PERIOD.

I WAS SURE OF IT.

SIZZLE
FLIP
AAAH
HEHEH
SMACK
AAGHHH!
THWACK!
YESSSS!
GOOD SHOT!

SIZZLE
SIZZLE
HAPPY BIRTHDAY! READY FOR SOME PANCAKES?
CAN WE GO NOW???
HAPPY BIRTHDAY!
COME ON! WE CAN EAT LATER.
JUST HAVE TO FINISH MY YOGA FIRST.
ALSO, IT'S NOT OPEN YET.
SIGH
ALL IN GOOD TIME, BIRTHDAY GIRL. EAT UP!
OKAAAY.

PUT ONE HAND ON YOUR BELLY...
SCARF SCARF
SCARF
AND ONE HAND OVER YOUR HEART...
SHHHWWW
BREATHE IN AND OUT...
GLUG GLUG GLUG
CLUNK
LET'S GO!
ALMOST DONE!

WOBBLE
THWUMP!
TAP
TAP
TAP
SIGH
NOM NOM
NOM NOM
SSSHHK
TRY TO APPRECIATE THIS MOMENT.
FEEL YOUR HEART EXPAND.

YOUR HEART'S EXPANDED ENOUGH, MOM! LET'S GO!
BRIIIING
HA HA HA
HA HA HA HA
GRANDMA WANTS TO KNOW WHAT TIME THE PARTY'S AT!
LET'S AIM FOR SIX O'CLOCK.
COME ON!

OF WISHING AND HOPING AND BEGGING...

AT LAST, I WAS GETTING MY VERY OWN DOG.

SURE, MOM AND DAD SAID THE DOG WOULD BELONG TO THE WHOLE FAMILY. BUT I KNEW BETTER.
AFTER ALL...
BURRRRP!
LIAM AND NOAH DIDN'T REALLY PAY ATTENTION TO ANYONE...
HA HA HA
HA HA HA
HA HA HA
BUT EACH OTHER.

THAT JUST MEANT THE DOG WOULD BE MINE.

ALL MINE.

REMEMBER, WE MIGHT NOT FIND THE RIGHT DOG ON THE FIRST VISIT. AND THEY MIGHT NOT HAVE ANY PUP—

I KNOW, I KNOW!

BUT THEY DID HAVE PUPPIES.
CLINIC
Welcome!
EMERGENCY & CLINIC
GROOMING CENTER
CAT WING
DOG WING
RESTROOMS
YIP YIP
YIP YIP YIP
YIP YIP YIP

WOULD YOU LIKE TO HOLD HIM?
LICK LICK

AND I FOUND THE RIGHT ONE RIGHT AWAY.

LOOKS LIKE WE'VE GOT OURSELVES A PUPPY.
...DOG OWNERSHIP... VACCINATIONS... PAPERWORK...
DOG OWNERSHIP!!!
THIS WAY, PLEASE.
FETCH!
BARK
BARK
ITCH ITCH
RUB RUB RUB

ALL I WANTED TO THINK ABOUT WAS MY PUPPY.

WHOA! SHE LOOKS LIKE SOMEONE PUNCHED HER IN THE FACE!
WHAT'S WRONG WITH HER?
LOOKS LIKE AN ALLERGIC REACTION!!
WE'D BETTER GET HER TO A DOCTOR!
EGHHH.

WE'LL BE BACK!
BUT WE NEVER DID GO BACK.
12
11
1
10
2
9
3
8
4
7
5
6
AND I DIDN'T GET MY PERFECT LITTLE PUPPY.
COOL PACK
10

Chapter Two

MAYBE IT WASN'T THE DOG. MAYBE I'M ALLERGIC TO SOMETHING ELSE. OR I JUST GOT SICK ALL OF A SUDDEN! IT COULD HAVE BEEN ANYTHING, REALLY, WHEN YOU THINK ABOUT IT.
FAMILY ALLERGY CENTER
WELL, IT WILL BE GOOD TO KNOW FOR SURE.
I WAS IN DENIAL.

OW
MEDICAL HISTORY. BOTH SIDES, PLEASE!

LET'S JUST GET THIS OVER WITH SO I CAN ADOPT MY DOG ALREADY.
WHAT ARE THEY GOING TO DO, ANYWAY?
THEY'LL PUT A LOT OF DIFFERENT THINGS THAT PEOPLE CAN BE ALLERGIC TO ON YOUR SKIN, AND THEN SEE WHAT YOU REACT TO.

SO THEY JUST PUT THEM ON MY SKIN? HOW?
WELL...IT'S JUST A TEENY TINY REALLY SMALL PRICK.
LIKE A SHOT?!
LIKE A BUNCH OF SHOTS AT THE SAME TIME?!
NO, NOT-
MARGARET WILSON?

I WANT YOU TO TAKE A DEEP BREATH...
OKAY, NOW BREATHE OUT...SLOWLY.
YOU'RE DOING GREAT.
NOT AS BAD AS A SHOT. KIND OF LIKE A SCRATCH OR A POKE.

BREATHE IN...
AND OUT.
THESE TWO ARE THE CONTROLS. YOU SHOULD REACT TO THE POSITIVE ONE, BUT NOT THE NEGATIVE ONE.
ALL FINISHED. I'LL BE BACK IN FIFTEEN MINUTES TO CHECK FOR REACTIONS. BE SURE NOT TO TOUCH THE TESTING AREA!
I BET I'M NOT GOING TO HAVE A SINGLE ALLERGY!

WANT ME TO READ TO YOU?
BUT WHAT IF I DO?
DON'T REACT...
SHAKE
I NEEDED TO CONCENTRATE ON STOPPING ANY POSSIBLE REACTIONS.
PLEASE...
ITCH
ITCH ITCH
ONE MINUTE
DON'T...
ITCH ITCH
ITCH ITCH
FIVE MINUTES
BE...
ITCH ITCH ITCH
TEN MINUTES
ALLERGIC!
ITCH ITCH
ITCH ITCH
ITCH ITCH ITCH
FIFTEEN MINUTES

LET'S SEE...YOU'VE HAD A VERY STRONG REACTION TO RABBITS... FEATHERS...COCKROACHES...CATS...
AND DOGS.
THE DOCTOR WILL BE IN SHORTLY TO DISCUSS YOUR RESULTS.

HELLO...
I'M DR. IDONIJE.
AND YOU MUST BE MAGGIE. MAY I TAKE A LOOK AT YOUR ARM?
ITCH ITCH
LOOKS LIKE SOME INTENSE ANIMAL ALLERGIES HERE. ANY PETS AT HOME?
ITCH ITCH
ITCH
NO.

OKAY, WE'VE GOT EVERYTHING RECORDED...
LET'S GO AHEAD AND MAKE YOU MORE COMFORTABLE. THIS ANTI-ITCH CREAM WILL HELP IF YOU HAVE ANY SKIN REACTIONS AGAIN. RASHES ARE UNUSUAL WITH PET ALLERGIES, BUT YOUR MOM MENTIONED THAT YOU HAD THAT RESPONSE BEFORE.
I'M UNUSUALLY ALLERGIC!
WHAT ABOUT OTHER PETS THAT WEREN'T ON THE TEST?
AH!
LIKE GUINEA PIGS AND HAMSTERS?
WITH THE TEST RESULTS SUGGESTING ALLERGIES TO SEVERAL KINDS OF ANIMALS ALREADY, YOU'LL WANT MAGGIE TO STAY AWAY FROM ANY WITH FUR OR FEATHERS.

WHAT ABOUT HYPOALLERGENIC DOGS?
SOME BREEDS SHED LESS THAN OTHERS, BUT NO DOG IS TRULY HYPOALLERGENIC.
AVOIDANCE ALTOGETHER IS REALLY THE BEST POLICY WITH THIS LEVEL OF REACTION.
BUT I DON'T UNDERSTAND! WHAT'S MAKING ME ALLERGIC?!

HERE'S HOW IT WORKS.
OUR BODIES EACH HAVE WHAT'S CALLED **AN IMMUNE SYSTEM** TO PROTECT AGAINST INVADERS...
LIKE BACTERIA OR VIRUSES.
WHEN YOU HAVE ALLERGIES, YOUR IMMUNE SYSTEM IS A LITTLE BIT, WELL, MIXED UP. INSTEAD OF PROTECTING YOU FROM ONLY HARMFUL SUBSTANCES...
IT ALSO TRIES TO PROTECT YOU FROM NORMALLY HARMLESS SUBSTANCES, LIKE, IN YOUR CASE, ANIMAL DANDER.
DANDER? WHAT'S DANDER? LIKE DANDRUFF?

DANDER IS MADE UP OF TINY FLAKES FROM ANIMAL SKIN. THE PROTEIN FOUND IN DANDER, SALIVA, AND URINE IS WHAT TRIGGERS ALLERGIC REACTIONS.
URINE?! EW!
I'M ALLERGIC TO ANIMAL PEE?
WELL, THAT'S PART OF IT.
THE COMIC IS YOURS TO KEEP. A NURSE WILL GIVE YOU A PACKET WITH MORE INFORMATION...
INCLUDING SOME PAPERWORK ABOUT ALLERGY SHOTS —
SHOTS?!
SOMETHING TO CONSIDER.

I'M SORRY, SWEETIE...DO YOU WANT TO TALK ABOUT IT?

I FELT LIKE MY BODY HAD DECIDED...
THAT ANIMALS...
WERE MY ENEMIES.
SLAM
SMACK
HOW COULD MY OWN BODY BE SO WRONG ABOUT ME?

R-R-R-RIP!
THUNK
CRASH
RIP
CRASH
NO FUR...NO FEATHERS...
HMM...

SCRTCH
SCRTCH
SCRTCH
PET POSSIBILITIES
NO FUR OR FEATHERS!
1. FISH
2. LIZARD
3. SNAKE
4. FROG/TOAD
5. TURTLE
6. TORTOISE
7. HERMIT CRAB
8. HEDGEHOG
9. TARANTULA?

THIS IS THE LIFE!
SNUFFLE
GLUB
GLUB
S-S-S-LITHER
CHIRP
CLICK
CLICK
RIB-BIT
RIB-BIT

Chapter Three

YE—
WE'LL SEE.
WHAT'S HAPPENING TO OUR CHILDREN?
DA-AAAD!
IT'S...IT'S CONTAGIOUS!
STOP IT!
IT'S...GOT...ME!
ME...TOO!

AGGHHH!
HA HA HA
HA
HA HA
OW! LIAM, YOU'RE ELBOWING ME!
REMEMBER TO USE YOUR WORDS, BOYS.

PET QUEST #1
HI, BLUEBELL!
YOU'RE SUCH A CUTE LITTLE FISHY...
SHAKE
SHAKE
YES YOU ARE...
GLUB
GLUB
BUT I WISH YOU COULD COME OUT OF THERE.
GOOD-BYE, DEAR BLUEBELL!
I SHOULD HAVE APPRECIATED HER MORE, GRANDMA!
SOB
SOB
FLUSH
PET POSSIBIL
NO FUR OR FEAT
1. FISH
2. LIZARD
3. SNAKE
4. FROG/TOAD
5. TURTLE
6. TORTOISE
7. HERMIT CRAB
8. HEDGE HOG

PET QUEST #2
GOT IT?
GOT IT!
COOL!
AWESOME!
IT'S OKAY. I WON'T HURT YOU, I PROMISE!
LET ME TRY!
ME TOO!
IT POOPED ON ME!
HA HA! MY TURN!
WHO WAS I TO STAND IN THE WAY OF TRUE LOVE?
THANKS, MAGGIE!
POSS
NO FUR OR
1. FISH
2. LIZARD
3. SNAKE
4. FROG/TOAD
TURTLE

PET QUEST #3
I AM NOT DOING THAT!
DID YOU KNOW?
WHEN FEEDING YOUR SNAKE
PET POSSIBILITIES
NO FUR OR FEATHER
1. FISH
2. LIZARD
3. SNAKE
4. FROG/TOAD
5. TURTLE
6. TORTOISE
7. HERMIT CRAB
8. HEDGEHOG
9. TARANTULA?
PET QUEST #4
CARING FOR YOUR FROG OR TOAD
DO NOT HANDLE OR TOUCH
WHAT?!
DO NOT HANDLE OR TOUCH
YOUR FROG OR TOAD UNLESS ABSOLUTELY NECESSARY!
PET POSSIBILITIES
NO FUR OR FEATHER
1. FISH
2. LIZARD
3. SNAKE
4. FROG/TOAD
5. TURTLE
6. TORTOISE
7. HERMIT CRAB
8. HEDGEHOG
9. TARANTULA?
PET QUEST #5
TURTLE
YOUR PET TURTLE WILL HIBERNATE FOR TWO TO FOUR MONTHS OF THE YEAR!
UGH!
PET POSSIBILITIES
NO FUR OR FEATHER
1. FISH
2. LIZARD
3. SNAKE
4. FROG/TOAD
5. TURTLE
6. TORTOISE
7. HERMIT CRAB
8. HEDGEHOG
9. TARANTULA?

PET QUEST #6
6
I'VE GOT IT! I'M GONNA GET A TORTOISE! THEY CAN LIVE FOR DECADES!
I LOVE YOUR ENTHUSIASM, BUT WE CAN'T COMMIT TO CARING FOR A PET THAT LONG.
2. LIZARD
3. SNAKE
4. FROG/TOAD
5. TURTLE
6. TORTOISE
7. HERMITCRAB
HEDGEHOG
TARANTULA?
PET QUEST #7
JUST SO YOU KNOW, I NEVER EVEN SAW IT MOVE.
2. LIZARD
3. SNAKE
4. FROG/TOAD
5. TURTLE
6. TORTOISE
7. HERMITCRAB
8. HEDGEHOG
9. TARANTULA
PET QUEST #8
HI. DO YOU SELL HEDGEHOGS?
HEDGEHOGS ARE ACTUALLY ILLEGAL IN CALIFORNIA—
ILLEGAL?!
2. LIZARD
3. SNAKE
4. FROG/TOAD
5. TURTLE
6. TORTOISE
7. HERMITCRAB
8. HEDGEHOG
9. TARANTULA

PET POSSIBILITIES
NO FUR OR FEATHERS!
1. FISH
2. LIZARD
3. SNAKE
4. FROG/TOAD
5. TURTLE
6. TORTOISE
7. HERMIT CRAB
8. HEDGEHOG
9. TARANTULA?
WHY'D I EVEN WRITE DOWN "TARANTULA"?! I DON'T WANT A SPIDER FOR A PET!
THIS IS IMPOSSIBLE!
PING

SCHOOL

Chapter Four

AND IT WAS GOING TO BE THE **WORST** DAY EVER.

I WAS SURE OF IT.

SPUTTER
SPLOOSH
HA HA HA HA
HOW CAN YOU BE LAUGHING? AREN'T YOU NERVOUS AT ALL?

NERVOUS?
ABOUT WHAT?
DON'T YOU CARE THAT WE HAVE TO GO TO A NEW SCHOOL? WHEN WE DIDN'T EVEN MOVE? IT'S NOT FAIR!
THEY CHANGED THE SCHOOL BOUNDARIES, MAGGIE.
YEAH, I HEARD ABOUT THAT, LIAM.
NOAH AND I ARE IN THE SAME CLASS! OUR FIRST TIME IN THE SAME CLASS!
NONE OF MY FRIENDS GOT SWITCHED TO GOLDEN RIVER.

BYE, MOM!
HAVE A GREAT FIRST DAY OF SCHOOL!
BUMP
WHOOPS!
SQUEEZE
I GOTTA GET GOING, SWEETIE, BUT GRANDMA WILL BE HERE WHEN YOU GET HOME.

REMEMBER — TAKE THOSE DEEP BREATHS IN AND OUT. YOU GOT THIS!
CLENCH
BREATHE IN...
AND OUT...

FIRST A NEW SCHOOL, AND THEN A NEW BABY. WHY COULDN'T THINGS JUST STAY THE SAME?
SOLD
SIT TOGETHER?
WATCH THIS!
NEW BACKPACK!
COOL SHOES!
HAD THAT TEACHER LAST YEAR...
CAN'T WAIT!
COME TO MY HOUSE AFTER SCHOOL?
SCHOOL

GOLDEN RIVER
ELEMENTARY
WELCOME
BACK
STUDENTS

YES! WE'RE IN THE SAME CLASS AGAIN!
YAY!
I WANT MY MOMMY!
HEY!
HA HA
OMIGOSH! I MISSED YOU SO MUCH!

?
WHAT DO YOU THINK IT IS?
A SNOW-CONE MACHINE!
A ROBOT THAT DOES HOMEWORK!
PRESENTS!
I WAS CURIOUS ABOUT THE BOX LIKE EVERYONE ELSE...

BUT I WAS WONDERING EVEN MORE IF ANY OF THESE UNFAMILIAR KIDS WOULD BECOME MY FRIENDS.
TAP TAP TAP
WELCOME TO THE FIFTH GRADE!
WE HAVE A FABULOUS NEW YEAR TO LOOK FORWARD TO, INCLUDING TIME WITH OUR VERY OWN...
CLASS PET!
PET?!

SWISH

MEET SPOTS!
OOOOOOOOOOOOOOOH!!
FEEL FREE TO COME UP AND TAKE A CLOSER LOOK.
HE'S ADORABLE!
THIS IS GONNA BE THE BEST YEAR EVER!
DO WE GET TO TAKE HIM HOME?
I'M IN LOVE.
UH-OH.
ACHOO!

ARE YOU OKAY?
ACHOO! ACHOO! ACHOO!
DON'T SNEEZE, DON'T SNEEZE, DON'T SNEEZE!
YES, I'M —
ACHOO!

YES, I SEE IT IN HER FILE, MRS. WILSON. THERE IT IS. ALLERGIC TO ANIMALS...YES...YES. WE'LL DEFINITELY TAKE CARE OF IT.
HOW ARE YOU FEELING?
DON'T LET THE GERMS SPREAD! WASH YOUR HANDS
What Hurts?

NOW EVERYONE'S GONNA HATE ME.

THE NEXT DAY
DUE TO UNFORESEEN CIRCUMSTANCES, SPOTS WILL BE MOVED TO MR. RICE'S CLASS...
WHERE YOU CAN VISIT HIM BEFORE SCHOOL AND DURING RECESS.
IT'S NOT MY FAULT THAT I'M ALLERGIC!
BUT IT FELT LIKE ALL MY FAULT.

WORST. DAY. EVER.
SCHOOL
SOLD
HEY!

HI! I'M CLAIRE!
OH...HI.
WHAT'S YOUR NAME?
MAGGIE.
I JUST MOVED IN! WANT TO COME OVER?
UM...
COME ON! I'LL SHOW YOU MY NEW ROOM! AND I BET I CAN GET MY DAD TO ORDER US SOME PIZZA.
OKAY! LET ME JUST TELL MY GRANDMA.

TODAY WAS MY FIRST DAY OF SCHOOL — I HAD TO MISS THE REAL FIRST DAY BECAUSE OUR MOVING TRUCK BROKE DOWN. ISN'T THAT THE WORST? I'M IN SIXTH GRADE. MY TEACHER'S **THE BEST.** HOW'S YOURS? OH, DO YOU LIKE PAINTING? MY DAD SAID I CAN PAINT ANYTHING I WANT ON THE WALLS. YOU CAN HELP ME! IT'S SO COOL THAT YOU LIVE NEXT DOOR. WE ARE GOING TO HAVE **SO. MUCH. FUN!**

Chapter Five

Maggie's House
BANG
BANG
BANG
HA HA HA HA
JUMP
JUMP
HA HA HA
WHIRR
CLUNK
CLACK
I LOVED HANGING OUT AT CLAIRE'S HOUSE. IT WAS SO DIFFERENT FROM MINE, AND MUCH MORE PEACEFUL.

LET'S GO BACK TO YOUR HOUSE! MINE'S **BORING.**
YOUR ROOM IS SO COOL.
THANKS! IT'S FUN HAVING A HOUSE AND KNOWING THINGS ARE GOING TO STAY THE WAY YOU MAKE THEM, YOU KNOW? WE'VE ALWAYS HAD APARTMENTS WITH ANNOYING RULES.
YOU UNPACKED SO FAST!
THAT'S BECAUSE OF MY DAD. WE'VE MOVED SO MANY TIMES, HE SAYS HE HAS IT DOWN TO A SCIENCE.
"THE MOST IMPORTANT THING IS TO GET PICTURES ON THE WALLS RIGHT AWAY. IF YOU DON'T, IT'LL NEVER GET DONE."
HA HA HA
MY PARENTS TAKE **FOREVER** TO DO STUFF. THEY'VE BEEN TELLING ME WE'LL GO TO THE BEACH FOR LIKE THREE YEARS, BUT WE NEVER GO!
YEAH, MY DAD CAN BE SLOW, TOO. HE SAID HE'LL HELP ME TURN THE SHED IN THE BACKYARD INTO A CLUBHOUSE...BUT IT MIGHT TAKE A WHILE.

. . .
SO, WHAT DO YOU WANT TO DO?
UM...
I KNOW! WE COULD BAKE SIX DIFFERENT KINDS OF CUPCAKES!
SURE...BUT WILL YOUR DAD LET US?
OH, HE DEFINITELY WILL. HE **HAS** TO.
HOW COME?
MY DAD PROMISED THAT IF I HAD A GOOD ATTITUDE ABOUT MOVING, THEN HE'D TRY HIS BEST TO ALWAYS...
"SAY YES TO THE MESS."

CAN MAGGIE AND I BAKE SIX KINDS OF CUPCAKES?
...YES!
CLATTER
CLATTER
WHISK...

WHY DID YOU MOVE, ANYWAY?
MY DAD QUIT HIS DAY JOB TO BE A FULL-TIME ARTIST. IT'S CHEAPER HERE.
CHEAP?! MY PARENTS ARE ALWAYS TALKING ABOUT HOW CALIFORNIA'S SO EXPENSIVE.
WELL, THEY SHOULD TRY LIVING IN THE CITY.
THE CITY? SACRAMENTO?
NO! SAN FRANCISCO.
OH...IS THAT WHERE YOU'RE FROM?
UH-HUH.
THAT'S SO COOL THAT YOUR DAD'S AN ARTIST.
WHAT DO YOUR PARENTS DO?
MY MOM'S A SOCIAL WORKER AND MY DAD'S A COMPUTER TECH FOR AN ENGINEERING COMPANY.
WHAT ABOUT YOU, WHAT DO YOU WANT TO BE WHEN YOU GROW UP?
I DON'T KNOW...I USED TO WANT TO BE A VET.
WELL, I THINK WE SHOULD OPEN A BAKERY TOGETHER 'CAUSE THESE ARE LOOKING **AMAZING**.
YUM!

CAN WE PAINT THE UPSTAIRS BATHROOM BLUE? CAN WE ADD A TREE TO THE DINING ROOM? GLUE FLOWERS TO THE KITCHEN CUPBOARDS? PUT A BOWLING ALLEY IN THE FAMILY ROOM???
UM, GREAT IDEAS, BUT WE'RE KIND OF RUNNING TWO STEPS BEHIND ALREADY.
WHY DON'T YOU START WITH BRAINSTORMING SOME IDEAS FOR YOUR ROOM?
FINE.

BUT I STILL DIDN'T KNOW WHAT TO DO WITH MY ROOM.
IT USED TO FEEL SO **ME**. BUT NOW...
SIGH.

I WISH FIFTH AND SIXTH GRADES HAD THE SAME LUNCHTIME...
ME TOO!

I HAD A LOT OF FRIENDS AT MY OLD SCHOOL.
IT SHOULD BE AGAINST THE LAW TO MAKE FIFTH GRADERS SWITCH SCHOOLS.
PUSH
SIXTH GRADERS...EEK!
OH...HI, CLAIRE!
PUSH
HEY! EVERYBODY, THIS IS MY NEXT-DOOR NEIGHBOR MAGGIE!
WHAT CLASS ARE YOU IN?
OMIGOSH! I'VE SEEN YOU BEFORE! YOU'RE IN MY LITTLE BROTHER'S CLASS!
WAIT, ISN'T HE IN FIFTH GRADE?
UM...
YOU'RE FRIENDS WITH A **FIFTH** GRADER?!
UH, **YEAH.** 'CAUSE SHE'S AWESOME.

BYE!
BYE, MAGGIE!

AT LEAST I HAD ONE BRAND-NEW PERFECT FRIEND.

CAN MAGGIE AND I HAVE A WATER BALLOON FIGHT?
GO FOR IT!
HEE HEE HEE
SPLASH
SPLASH
SPLASH
HA HA HA HA
GRAAANDMA!!!

CAN MAGGIE AND I BUILD A FORT?
OF COURSE!
LIAM AND NOAH WOULD DESTROY THIS IN LIKE TWO SECONDS.
I BET...THEY ARE REALLY CUTE, THOUGH.
CUTE?! MORE LIKE ANNOYING! AND NOW THERE'S GONNA BE A BABY TO TORTURE ME, TOO!
DON'T YOU THINK IT MIGHT BE KIND OF...I DON'T KNOW, FUN? HAVING A NEW BABY?

NO WAY! MY FAMILY'S BIG ENOUGH ALREADY.
OH, SURE...
LET'S SECRET SWAP!
OKAY.
IT DOESN'T HAVE TO BE A **SECRET** SECRET. JUST SOMETHING WE DON'T KNOW ABOUT EACH OTHER.
I'LL GO FIRST. UM...
MY PARENTS ARE DIVORCED AND MY MOM LIVES IN NEW YORK. I VISIT HER EVERY SUMMER. AND SOMETIMES FOR HOLIDAYS.
OH.

YOU GO TO NEW YORK EVERY SUMMER? THAT'S SO COOL!
HAVE YOU EVER BEEN?
NEVER.
FWUMP
OKAY — YOUR TURN.
UM...OKAY. HERE'S MINE...
I'M ALLERGIC TO ANIMALS.
SERIOUSLY?!
YEAH...BUT I'M GONNA START ALLERGY SHOTS SOON...
OH, I JUST REMEMBERED! DO YOU WANT TO COME TO MY FAMILY'S MOVIE NIGHT ON FRIDAY?
UH, DEFINITELY!

FRIDAY NIGHT
CRASH!
BANG!
OOH, THE BABY'S KICKING!
HEE HEE HEE
QUICK!

WHOA...
YOU KNOW, WHEN I WAS PREGNANT WITH YOU, HANNAH, YOU WOULD NOT STOP HICCUPING. ESPECIALLY WHEN I WAS TRYING TO SLEEP — IT WAS NOTHING BUT **HICCUP, HICCUP** ALL NIGHT.
AND NOW SHE DOESN'T STOP SNORING...
GIGGLE
THWUMP!
HEY, PLAY NICE, YOU TWO!
ARGHHH
HA HA HA
HA HA HA
DING-DONG!
KICK

PLEASE BE CLAIRE...
YAY! I'M SO GLAD YOU'RE HERE!
WHISPER WHISPER

I'D SAVED UP MY OWN MONEY TO BUY A SURPRISE FOR CLAIRE.

WHAT?!
LICK
ISN'T HE THE CUTEST?!
YIP YIP
HOW COULD SHE?
MAGGIE?

SNAP

Chapter Six

A PUPPY!
YOU GOT A DOG?!
ISN'T HE THE CUTEST EVER! CAN YOU GET MAGGIE? I CAN'T WAIT TO SHOW HER.
MAGGIE!! CLAIRE'S HERE!!
AROOOOOO!!
OW!
THIS END UP

THEY WERE **TRAITORS.** ALL OF THEM.

UH...TOO MUCH HOMEWORK!
OH, OKAY...
CAN I PET HIM?
CAN WE PLAY WITH HIM?
UM...
SURE! COME ON, I CAN TAKE HIM OFF HIS LEASH IN MY BACKYARD.
MAGGIE! COME OVER WHEN YOU FINISH YOUR HOMEWORK!
GRANDMA!!! WE'RE GOING TO CLAIRE'S!
OKAY! HAVE FUN!

HE'S FUZZY!
YOU'RE SO LUCKY!
THAT'S WHAT I'M NAMING HIM — LUCKY!
SOME PEOPLE HAD IT ALL.
SNAP
RUFF RUFF RUFF
BA-BUMP BA-BUMP BA-BUMP
I WAS NEVER GOING TO BE ABLE TO GET A PUPPY... AND NOW I DIDN'T HAVE A BEST FRIEND, EITHER.

KNOCK! KNOCK!
MAGGIE, SWEETIE, CLAIRE'S HERE.
STUDYING!
MAGGIE? CLAIRE'S AT THE DOOR.
NOT FEELING WELL!
CLAIRE WANTS YOU TO GO TO THE MOVIES WITH HER.
I'M ASLEEP.
MAYBE SHE'LL TAKE US INSTEAD...
HEY, NO FAIR!
UGHHHHH.
MAGGIE, ARE YOU OKAY?

CAN I GET A PUPPY?
SURE! OF COURSE! **ANYTHING FOR YOU!** OTHER PEOPLE HAVE TO WAIT AND WISH AND DREAM FOR THINGS.
BUT YOU ALWAYS GET **ANYTHING** YOU **EVER** WANT RIGHT AWAY!!
TIME TO GET READY FOR SCHOOL!
SCHOOL?! OH NO!!
HOW WOULD I AVOID CLAIRE ON THE BUS?

CAN YOU PLEASE DRIVE ME?
YOU KNOW YOU NEED TO TAKE THE BUS, SWEETIE!
BUT YOU'LL GET A RIDE HOME TODAY. DAD'S PICKING YOU UP EARLY FOR YOUR SHOT, REMEMBER?

SHOT?!
YOUR ALLERGY SHOT.
THAT'S TODAY?!

NED, DON'T FORGET TO REMIND HER TO DO THE DEEP BREATHING WE'VE BEEN WORKING ON.
THE ALLERGY SHOTS WEREN'T GOING TO MAKE ME COMPLETELY **NOT** ALLERGIC. I STILL WOULDN'T BE ABLE TO GET A DOG.
GOT IT!
BUT THEY WOULD **HOPEFULLY** STOP ME FROM GETTING AS SICK AROUND OTHER PEOPLE'S PETS.
YOU KNOW...SOME EXPERTS SAY THAT ICE CREAM SPEEDS UP THE ALLERGY SHOT RECOVERY PROCESS.
OOH, BRING HOME SOME PISTACHIO FOR THE PREGNANT LADY, PLEASE!

MUST...AVOID...CLAIRE!
PANT
PANT
PANT
TAP
TAP
HEY!
THWUMP

PLEASE SEND MARGARET WILSON TO THE OFFICE. HER FATHER'S WAITING.
H-HI.
SIGH

HEY, IT'S MY TROOPER!
MY FAVORITE DAUGHTER!
NUDGE
PUSH

SLIDE
WHAT'S THAT?!
OH, THAT! I THOUGHT SOMETHING BAD HAD HAPPENED!

SOMETHING BAD **WAS** HAPPENING, EVEN IF MOM AND DAD THOUGHT IT WAS GOOD.

MARGARET?

DID YOU TAKE YOUR ALLERGY MEDICATION?
YES.
EEEEEEK!
DON'T WORRY — THIS WILL BE OVER BEFORE YOU KNOW IT.
OUCH

NOW ON TO ARM TWO! ALMOST FINISHED...
PLEASE INFORM A NURSE IMMEDIATELY IF YOU HAVE AN ABNORMAL REACTION
NORMAL REACTIONS
• swelling • redness
• irritation at the injection site
ABNORMAL REACTIONS
• sneezing • nasal congestion
• hives • chest tightening • coughing
wheezing • difficulty breathing
• swelling beyond the site of the injection
• rapid heartbeat • weak pulse • fainting
• dizziness • vomiting • diarrhea
• sense of impending doom
SENSE OF IMPENDING DOOM??
WAIT FOR A HALF HOUR AND ALERT THE FRONT DESK IMMEDIATELY IF YOU EXPERIENCE ANY ABNORMAL REACTIONS.

I FORGOT TO REMIND YOU ABOUT THE DEEP BREA—
WHAT'S SENSE OF IMPENDING DOOM MEAN?
HUH?
IT WAS ON THE LIST OF POSSIBLE BAD REACTIONS TO THE SHOT.
OH. HUH. YEAH, I SAW THAT, TOO.
I GUESS IT'S A FEELING THAT SOMETHING REALLY BAD IS GOING TO HAPPEN. "DOOM" MEANS SOMETHING, WELL, REALLY, REALLY BAD HAPPENING. AND "IMPENDING" MEANS IT'S GOING TO HAPPEN SOON.
YOU FEEL OKAY? ANY SENSE OF IMPENDING DOOM?
NAH, I'M OKAY.
ITCH ITCH ITCH
BUT I COULDN'T STOP WONDERING: WHAT WAS IT CALLED WHEN THE BAD THING HAD ALREADY HAPPENED?

SUNNY'S ICE CREAM
SPECIALS!

Chapter Seven

AGHHHH!!!
I CAN'T TAKE IT ANYMORE!
SCRATCH SCRATCH SCRATCH
SCRATCH .. SCRATCH .. SCRATCH
BARK .. BARK
ANY OF IT.

WOOOSH
I'LL BE DEFENSE!
BARK
BARK
BARK
I'LL BE OFFENSE!

QUIET, LUCKY.
BARK BARK BARK
SNIFF SNIFF
IT'S GONNA BE OKAY.
SOB SOB
SOB SOB
SOB SOB
SOB
SOB SOB SOB

WHOA! I WONDER WHAT'S WRONG.

KICK
WAS SHE CRYING BECAUSE OF...ME?
WHACKK
SORRY!
OUCH
IT HADN'T OCCURRED TO ME THAT MAYBE I WASN'T THE ONLY ONE WHO MISSED BEING FRIENDS...
AFTER ALL, NOW THAT CLAIRE HAD LUCKY FOR COMPANY, WHY WOULD SHE NEED ME?

BA-BUMP BA-BUMP BA-BUMP BA-BUMP
BA-BUMP
BA-BUMP
BA-BUMP
BA-BUMP
RUFF RUFF
SHAKE
KNOCK KNOCK

OH...
IT'S YOU.
I'M SORRY!!!
SQUEEEEEZE!
ACHOO!

I DON'T GET WHY YOU JUST...
DROPPED ME.
I WAS REALLY...MAD THAT YOU GOT A DOG EVEN THOUGH I TOLD YOU I WAS ALLERGIC. NOW I CAN'T EVEN COME TO YOUR HOUSE!
BUT YOU SAID YOU WERE STARTING ALLERGY SHOTS! AND IT'S NOT LIKE IT'S YOUR DOG.
I KNOW IT'S NOT MY DOG!!
BREATHE IN...

THE ALLERGY SHOTS TAKE A FEW MONTHS TO START WORKING. I HAVE TO GET THEM FOR FIVE YEARS.
OH. WOW.
AND THEY STILL WON'T CURE ME. JUST MAKE ME LESS ALLERGIC.
STAY, LUCKY.
SO YOU CAN'T COME TO MY HOUSE ANYMORE?
NOT REALLY. JUST FOR A FEW MINUTES AT A TIME.

UNLESS YOU TAKE LUCKY BACK?
GOOD ONE!
HA HA HA
WANT TO COME TO MY HOUSE?
THANKS FOR CHANGING FIRST!
NO PROBLEM...I WAS **COVERED** IN DOG HAIR!
YOU'RE THE BEST.

...WHAT THEY DO IS GIVE YOU A SHOT WITH A TINY BIT OF THE THING YOU'RE ALLERGIC TO IN IT. AND THEN THEY ADD MORE AND MORE OVER TIME, TO BUILD UP YOUR IMMUNE SYSTEM.
UGH, THAT SOUNDS **HORRIBLE!** I HATE SHOTS.
IT'S NOT **THAT** BAD.

MAYBE YOU CAN GET A DIFFERENT KIND OF PET?
CAN'T. I'VE TRIED LIZARDS AND STUFF. BUT NOTHING'S WORKED OUT. AND I REALLY JUST WANT A FURRY PET.
THE DOCTOR SAID I'M PROBABLY ALLERGIC TO ALL ANIMALS WITH FUR OR FEATHERS.
JUST PROBABLY?
YEAH. THEY CAN'T TEST FOR EVERY SINGLE ONE.
IF THEY DIDN'T TEST YOU FOR ALL ANIMALS, HOW CAN THEY KNOW FOR SURE?
MIX

HMM...
DO YOU THINK MAYBE IF THE FURRY ANIMAL WAS REALLY, REALLY, **REALLY** SMALL...
For Claire
YOU MIGHT NOT BE ALLERGIC TO IT?

PET QUEST #9
PET STO
2:15
SMALL MAMMALS
DING
DING DING
DO YOU THINK YOU HAVE ENOUGH?
ALMOST.
THERE. THAT SHOULD DO IT.
THANKS!

DO NOT DISTURB
PLEASE KNOCK
HA HA HA
HEY!
WHATCHA DOIN'?
NONE OF YOUR BUSINESS!
CAN I GET A LOCK FOR MY DOOR? PLEASE??

...GETTING OLDER...
...PRIVACY...
LOCK SAFE
JUST REMEMBER THAT YOUR MOM AND GRANDMA AND I CAN OPEN YOUR DOOR, TOO. BUT IF YOU'RE RESPONSIBLE, WE'LL RESPECT YOUR PRIVACY AND ONLY USE IT IN AN EMERGENCY.
OKAY!

SATURDAY
DAD'S TAKING THE BOYS TO THE PARK AND I'VE GOT ERRANDS TO RUN — WANT TO COME WITH ME?
THAT'S OKAY! I'M GOING TO CLAIRE'S HOUSE!
WOOSH

CAN YOU TAKE US TO THE PET STORE?
HMM...I COULD USE A BREAK...
HMM...
SURE!

FISH
SMALL MAMMALS→

SMALL MAMMALS
AWWWW!
SQUEAK
THANK YOU FOR HELPING ME! YOU'RE THE BEST!
PET SUPPLY

OH NO!
WHAT?
MY MOM'S BACK ALREADY!
DON'T WORRY! I'LL DISTRACT HER.
SOOO...WHAT BABY NAMES ARE YOU CONSIDERING?
WELL, I DO FIND IT HARD TO DECIDE BEFORE THE BABY'S —
RATTLE RATTLE
DID YOU HEAR THAT?
WHERE'S MAGGIE?
UM... ALREADY UPSTAIRS!
GOOD TALKING TO YOU!

MISSION ACCOMPLISHED!

YOU ARE THE **CUTEST**!
I WONDER...WHAT SHOULD I
NAME YOU?

SUGAR
COCOA
LUNA
DAISY
PIPSQUEAK
MOUSEY

Chapter Eight

CARING FOR YOUR PET MOUSE
TAMING YOUR PET MOUSE
1 At first, simply sit by your mouse's cage so they can get used to your presence.
RUB RUB
I WONDER IF SHE'S USED TO ME BY NOW...
RUB RUB
HOW WILL I KNOW WHEN SHE IS?
SNIFF SNIFF

TIME TO GET THIS PLACE CLEANED UP!
AND MAKE SURE YOU'RE AS COMFORTABLE AS POSSIBLE, LITTLE PIPSQUEAK!
ACHOO! ACHOO! ACHOOOOOO!!!!
SQUEAK!
DASH
UGH...I CAN BEAT THIS! SHE'S JUST A LITTLE MOUSE!
SHHHHHH
SCRUB
SCRUB
SCRUB

HERE, PIP-PIP. THIS IS FOR YOU!
SNIFF SNIFF
THAT'S RIGHT.
CRUNCH!
HERE'S SOME MORE...
SNIFF
SNIFF SNIFF
MUNCH! MUNCH!
GREAT JOB!

THAT TICKLES!
GIGGLE GIGGLE
HERE YOU GO. GOOD LITTLE PIPSQUEAK.
SHE'S ADORABLE!!!
SHE'S THE BEST!
THE BEST PET EVER.

AND SO:
ACHOO!
ACHOO!
ACHOO!
ACHOO!
ACHOOOO!!!

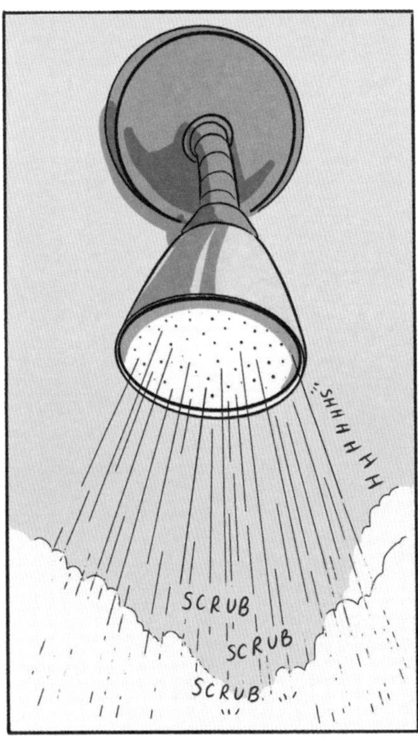
SHHHHHH
SCRUB
SCRUB
SCRUB

ITCH
ITCH
ITCH
ITCH
ITCH

CAN'T SCRATCH.
RUB RUB
SNIFF SNIFF
WHAT'S GOING ON? DID THEY BRING THAT GUINEA PIG BACK INTO YOUR CLASS?
OH...I THINK I'M JUST GETTING A COLD.
HMM...

KNOCK KNOCK KNOCK
LET US IN!
YOU'RE ALWAYS IN YOUR ROOM NOW!
JUST A MINUTE, PIP-PIP.
SLIDE
WHAT DO YOU WANT?
HEY, WHAT'S THAT SME—
WHOA! YOUR EYES ARE ALL RED!
YOU HAVE MONSTER EYES!

GO. AWAY!
SLAM
OOOH! I WANT MONSTER EYES!
GRAAAAANDMA! MAGGIE HAS MONSTER EYES.
HMM...
THAT NIGHT
I DO THINK YOU'D BETTER CALL THE ALLERGIST, DEAR.
I WONDER IF IT'S FROM THE SHOTS. SOME KIND OF REACTION.

THE NEXT DAY
SNIFFLE SNIFFLE
H-HI.

IS IT...IS IT OKAY IF I SIT HERE?
UH...SURE.
DO YOU WANT HALF MY COOKIE?
CAN'T. I'M ALLERGIC. THANKS, THOUGH!
DID YOU SAY **ALLERGIC**?
YEAH.

HOW COME YOU'RE NOT AT THE PEANUT-FREE TABLE?
I'M NOT ALLERGIC TO PEANUTS.
OH.
I'M ALLERGIC TO EGGS.
I HAVE ALLERGIES, TOO.
I KNOW.
HOW?
I'M IN MR. RICE'S CLASS. WE GOT SPOTS.
I GUESS EVERYONE KNOWS IT WAS MY FAULT.
IT WASN'T YOUR FAULT. YOU DON'T GET TO CHOOSE YOUR ALLERGIES.
MY NAME'S SEBASTIAN.
...I'M MAGGIE.

SO...ARE YOU JUST ALLERGIC TO GUINEA PIGS?
NO, ALL ANIMALS WITH FUR OR FEATHERS.
WOW, THAT'S HORRIBLE!
EXCEPT MICE... RIGHT?
WHAT ABOUT YOU? JUST EGGS?
JUST EGGS.
DO YOU HAVE TO GET ALLERGY SHOTS?
NAH. THEY DON'T WORK FOR FOOD ALLERGIES...
I'M NOT SURE WHY, ACTUALLY. I'LL HAVE TO LOOK THAT UP. ARE YOU GETTING THEM?
YEAH. THEY'RE... OKAY, I GUESS.

I'LL TELL MY SISTER. SHE'S ALLERGIC TO BEE STINGS — THEY HAVE SHOTS FOR THAT, TOO.
NOM NOM
NOM NOM
SO DO YOU HAVE AN EPIPEN?
NO. I GET REALLY BAD REACTIONS, BUT NOT ANA...ANAPH...THAT THING WHERE YOU HAVE TO USE AN EPIPEN.
ANAPHYLAXIS?
YEAH. ANAPHA...THAT.
HAVE YOU HAD IT?

ONCE. IT WAS...SCARY. I COULDN'T BREATHE RIGHT. I HAD TO GO TO THE HOSPITAL.
WHOA...THAT IS SCARY.
DO YOU ALWAYS CARRY AN EPIPEN AROUND?
YEP. HERE IT IS. NEVER LEAVE HOME WITHOUT IT.
WOW. THAT STINKS.
I'M GLAD I DON'T HAVE TO DO THAT.
EH. I'M USED TO IT. DID YOU HAVE TO GET RID OF ANY PETS WHEN YOU FOUND OUT?
SORT OF. I WAS GOING TO GET A PUPPY —
RIIIINGG
WELL, SEE YOU.
BYE.

HERE, PIP-PIP!
PIPSQUEAK? I'VE GOT A CARROT, YOUR FAVORITE!
HUH...MAYBE I'VE BEEN FEEDING YOU TOO MUCH?

THE NEXT MORNING
KNOCK KNOCK!
RISE AND SHINE, SWEETIE!
RUB RUB
I'M –
UP!
THUNK!

SLIDE
PIPSQUEAK?
PIP-PIP?
WHERE **ARE** YOU?

GASP!

SQUEAK

Chapter Nine

YOU'RE NOT GOING TO BELIEVE THIS...
SH SH SH SH SH
OMIGOSH, OMIGOSH, OMIGOSH!!! **NO WAY!**
WHOOSH!
WHOOSH
SHHHH!

Do not touch the baby mice for at least two weeks.
Continue to quietly provide food and fresh water.
TWO WEEKS?
THAT'S FOREVER!
At three weeks, separate the baby mice into male and female groups.
WHERE AM I GOING TO PUT ANOTHER CAGE?!
I KNOW! I CAN KEEP HALF OF THEM AT MY HOUSE! THE BOY ONES, SO YOU CAN KEEP PIPSQUEAK. I'M SURE MY DAD WILL LET ME.
I'M SURE HE WILL...
I GUESS...
OKAY.

OCTOBER
SUNDAY
MONDAY
TUESDAY
WEDNESDAY
THURSDAY
FRIDAY
SATURDAY
1
2
3
4
5
6
7
8
9
10
11
12
13
14
15
16
17
18
19
20
21
22
23
24
25
26
27
28
29
30
31
BABY DUE DATE

DON'T MAKE A SOUND...
TIP TOE
TIP TOE
TIP TOE
TIP TOE
ACHOO!
SLIDE
LOCK
SUNDAY MONDAY TUESDAY WEDNESDAY THURSDAY FRIDAY SATURDAY
BABY DUE DATE

SHHHHHHHH
SCRUB
SCRUB
SCRUB
BLIP!
BLINK
BLIP
BLINK
SUNDAY MONDAY TUESDAY WEDNESDAY THURSDAY FRIDAY SATURDAY
BABY DUE DATE

DO YOU THINK THE SHOTS ARE CAUSING IT?
SHE SHOULDN'T BE HAVING THIS LEVEL OF REACTION.
ARE YOU TAKING YOUR ALLERGY MEDICINE BEFORE EACH APPOINTMENT?
Y-YES.
OKAY, LET'S SLOW DOWN THE SHOT SCHEDULE AND TRY A DIFFERENT MEDICATION.
PHEW...
SUNDAY MONDAY TUESDAY WEDNESDAY THURSDAY FRIDAY SATURDAY
BABY DUE DATE

GOT ANY GOOD FACTS? I'M MAKING A BOOK OF MY FAVORITE TRIVIA.
GREAT IDEA!
UM...CALIFORNIA USED TO BE UNDERWATER?
ARE YOU ASKING, OR IS THAT A FACT?
IT'S A FACT.
COOL.
I WISH WE WERE UNDERWATER RIGHT NOW...OR AT LEAST AT THE BEACH.
TOO BAD WE'RE NOT CLOSER. IN MOVIES, EVERYONE IN CALIFORNIA ALWAYS LIVES RIGHT BY THE BEACH!
THE LAST TIME I WENT TO THE BEACH, IT WAS SO FOGGY I COULDN'T EVEN SEE THE OCEAN!
LAST TIME I WENT, WE WERE STUCK IN TRAFFIC FOR LIKE FIVE HOURS.
SEBASTIAN & MAGGIE'S BIG BOOK OF TRIVIA
* CALIFORNIA USED TO BE UNDERWATER
FACT: NOT EVERYONE IN CALIFORNIA LIVES BY THE BEACH
FACT: NORTHER
CALIFORNIA
BE COLD AND FOGGY EVEN IN THE SUMMER
4
5
6
11
12
13

OKAY, EVERYONE! I MADE SNICKERDOODLES.
OH, I'M NOT HUNGRY...
THEY ARE DELICIOUS, IF I DO SAY SO MYSELF.
BUT THEY'RE SNICKERDOODLES!
I'LL BE IN MY ROOM!
YOU'RE ALWAYS IN YOUR ROOM!
MY, MY, I NEVER THOUGHT I'D SEE THE DAY WHEN A GRANDCHILD OF MINE COULD RESIST A SNICKERDOODLE STRAIGHT FROM THE OVEN...
ARE YOU GETTING THAT THING?
BUT TO EACH HER OWN.
WHAT THING?

YOU KNOW, THAT THING. WHAT'S IT CALLED?
SH SH SH SH SH SH SH SH
OH YEAH!
PUBERTY!
WHAT?! NO!
NOW, BOYS, GIVE YOUR SISTER SOME SPACE.
AAHHH!
SNICKER SNICKER
SUNDAY MONDAY TUESDAY WEDNESDAY THURSDAY FRIDAY SATURDAY
BABY DUE DATE

OKAY, SO WE'VE GOT SUGAR, COCOA, LUNA, DAISY, MARSHMALLOW, BUBBLES, OTIS, PIXIE, BANDIT, AND ED...
WE JUST NEED ONE MORE! I REALLY LIKE JUNE...BUT IT JUST DOESN'T SEEM LIKE A MOUSE NAME, YOU KNOW?
BOUNCE
WHAT ABOUT MAX?
HMM...LET'S ADD IT TO THE LIST!
BORRRRING...

I'VE GOT SOME SUPER-WEIRD ALLERGY TRIVIA TO ADD!
OOOH, WHAT?
DID YOU KNOW THAT DOGS AND CATS CAN BE ALLERGIC TO **EACH OTHER?** AND THAT THEY CAN BOTH BE ALLERGIC TO **HUMANS?**
WHAT? REALLY?!
OCTOBER
15
16
17
22
23
24
I MISSED HOLDING PIPSQUEAK SO MUCH. I COULDN'T WAIT UNTIL THE MORNING, WHEN I COULD HOLD HER **AND** HER BABIES!

16
17
23
24
BUT I WOKE UP LATE...
BREAKFAST IS READY!
MAGGIE?
SLIDE
AWWW!
MAGGIE? ARE YOU UP?
COMING!
I'LL SEE YOU **RIGHT** AFTER SCHOOL!
PUSH
CLICK

ONLY TWO MORE WEEKS. CAN YOU BELIEVE IT? REALLY, IT COULD BE ANY DAY NOW.
TOO BAD IT'S NOT TWINS.
YEAH! THEN THERE'D BE ONE FOR EACH OF US.
YOU HEAR THAT, SWEETIE?
WHAT?

FEEL FREE TO SHOW UP ANY DAY NOW.
HEY!
OUCH OUCH
I'M SWEETIE!
STOMP STOMP
PING.

I CAN'T BELIEVE THE BABY MIGHT COME ANY DAY NOW! UGH!
I THINK IT'S COOL. I'VE ALWAYS WANTED –
THAT'S 'CAUSE YOU DON'T LIVE WITH LIAM AND NOAH!
ANYWAY... ARE YOU EXCITED ABOUT THE...
OTHER BABIES?
SO EXCITED!
YOU **HAVE** TO COME OVER RIGHT AFTER SCHOOL.
OF COURSE!!

TAP TAP
TAP TAP
DID YOU KNOW THAT THE HUMAN HEART BEATS ABOUT 100,000 TIMES EACH DAY?
TAP TAP
TAP TAP
TAP
HMM? OH... INTERESTING —
ACHOO!

DID YOU KNOW THAT I HAVE A SECRET PET MOUSE?
SO **THAT'S** WHY YOU'RE ALWAYS SNEEZING! COME ON, MAGGIE, YOU'RE **ALLERGIC.** I CAN'T EAT EGGS NO MATTER HOW MUCH I WANT TO!
FACTS ARE FACTS, MAGGIE! YOU CAN'T OUTSMART SCIENCE!
DON'T LISTEN TO HIM, MAGGIE! YOU LOVE ME AND I LOVE YOU AND ALL MY CHILDREN WILL LOVE YOU, TOO. THAT'S ALL THAT MATTERS.
RIIIIIING!
JUMP

BOUNCE
BOUNCE
BOUNC
I'M JUST GONNA DROP OFF MY BACKPACK!
WHOOSH
WHOOSH
TAP
TAP TAP

CAN'T WAIT...CAN'T WAIT...
CAN'T WAIT!
GRAAAANDMA!!
MAGGIE HAS TWELVE —
MICE IN HER ROOM!

BLINK
BLINK
AAAAAAA!
AAGHHHH!
AHHHH!!!!!

Chapter Ten

THIS IS YOUR FAULT, TOO! IT WAS YOUR IDEA IN THE FIRST PLACE!
BUT...BUT...
I'M **ALLERGIC**, CLAIRE! I CAN'T HAVE A PET LIKE YOU –
I CAN'T GET **EVERYTHING** I WANT LIKE YOU!
I WAS ONLY TRYING TO HELP!
SLAM!
MAGGIE'S ROOM
KEEP OUT!
SOB
SOB

I TALKED TO THE PET STORE. THEY'LL TAKE THEM ALL BACK.
IT WAS IRRESPONSIBLE OF THEM TO SELL A PREGNANT MOUSE IN THE FIRST PLACE! AND TO A CHILD!
THAT NIGHT
YEAH...POOR GIRL.
AT LEAST WE KNOW WHY HER ALLERGIES HAVE BEEN ACTING UP SO MUCH. I'VE BEEN SO WORRIED.
I JUST...I WISH I COULD MAKE IT BETTER.
SHE'S ALWAYS LOVED ANIMALS SO MUCH...

CONTRACTION?
HERE COMES ANOTHER — OH!
...AAAND DONE. WHEW! THAT WAS A STRONG ONE.
WELL, BETTER GET THIS TAKEN CARE OF. I'LL GO...

SLIDE
SQUEAK
SQUEAK
GOOD-BYE.
SQUEAK

GOOD-BYE, PIPSQUEAK AND SUGAR AND COCOA AND LUNA AND DAISY AND MARSHMALLOW AND BUBBLES AND OTIS AND PIXIE AND BANDIT AND ED. AND THE LAST BABY. I'M SORRY YOU DIDN'T GET A NAME.
SIGH
YOUR MOM AND I... IT'S OUR JOB TO TAKE CARE OF YOU. AND PART OF THAT IS KEEPING YOU HEALTHY.
YOU DON'T UNDERSTAND!
I'M TRYING TO, KIDDO... I WISH IT DIDN'T HAVE TO BE THIS WAY.

I JUST...
YES?
I WANTED A PET THAT WOULD LOVE ME MOST OF ALL! YOU AND MOM HAVE EACH OTHER AND THE BABY. NOAH AND LIAM ARE TWINS! I DON'T HAVE ANYONE THAT'S JUST MINE.
BUT...

THAT SOUNDS REALLY FRUSTRATING.
ALL I KNOW IS, I'M GLAD YOU'RE PART OF OUR FAMILY. DON'T KNOW WHAT WE'D DO WITHOUT YOU.
SQUEEZE...
AT LEAST I'M NOT ALLERGIC TO HUMANS.

FAR FROM IT! YOU'RE GOING TO BE GREAT WITH THE NEW BABY. YOU HELPED OUT SO MUCH WHEN LIAM AND NOAH WERE BORN.
I DID?
YEP. TODDLING AROUND, THROWING DIAPERS AWAY, GETTING BINKIES OFF THE FLOOR...
IT WAS SO SWEET.
WELL, AS MUCH AS I DON'T WANT TO DO THIS, IT'S TIME TO GET THOSE MICE BACK TO THE PET STORE BEFORE IT CLOSES.
I COULDN'T STAND TO SAY GOOD-BYE ALL OVER AGAIN.

CLICK

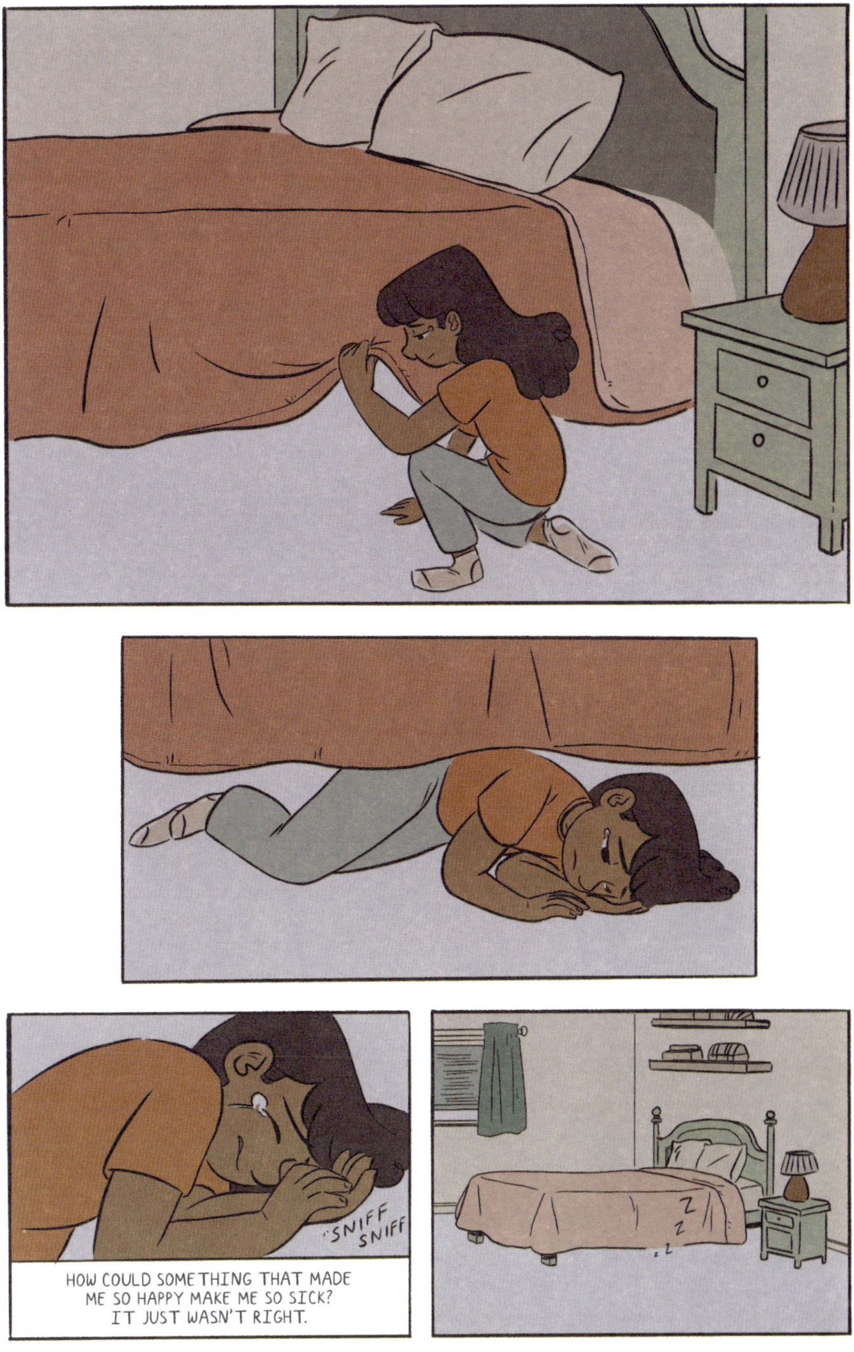
SNIFF
SNIFF
HOW COULD SOMETHING THAT MADE ME SO HAPPY MAKE ME SO SICK? IT JUST WASN'T RIGHT.
Z
Z
Z

THE NEXT MORNING
BANG!
BONK!
OW!
THERE YOU ARE! GUESS WHAT, GUESS WHAT, GUESS WHAT?
GO AWAY!

GRANDMA'S COMING OVER 'CAUSE THE BABY MIGHT BE BORN TODAY!
BONK!
I SAID GO AWAY!
BUT IT'S THIRTEEN DAYS EARLY!

MAGGIE
DEER MAGGIE, SRRY
Abt YR MISE ME
AND NOAH R SO
DAZILIUN MILLUN
TMES SRRY WE TULD ON
YU. WE LUV YU! LUV, LIAM AND NOAH
AW, HIS SPELLING IS KIND OF CUTE...
THE LITTLE TRAITOR.

I DON'T WANT YOU TO GO.
ZIIIIIP
I KNOW...
I'LL BE BACK SOON.
BUT IT WON'T BE THE SAME.
YOU NEVER KNOW...MAYBE IT WILL BE EVEN BETTER.
YEAH, RIGHT.

BYE!
COME BACK SOON!
DON'T FORGET THE BABY!
OH!
WAIT!
SCREECH!
MAGGIE?
DON'T FORGET TO TAKE DEEP BREATHS. IN AND OUT, OKAY?
NOD NOD

GRAAANDMA! NOAH ELBOWED ME!
GRAAANDMA! LIAM'S RIBS ARE POKING MY ELBOW!
SOUNDS LIKE YOUR ELBOWS AND RIBS NEED TO LEARN HOW TO GET ALONG!
WHAT IF SOMETHING GOES WRONG?
WHAT IF SOMETHING HAPPENS TO MOM?

MAGGIE? HELLO? ARE YOU AWAKE?
HUH?
EARTH TO MAGGIE!
SORRY, SEBASTIAN. WHAT WERE YOU SAYING?
RIIING

BRIIIIIING!
MM-HMM...OKAY...I SEE. THANKS FOR THE UPDATE.
EVERYTHING'S GOING FINE. JUST SLOWER THAN THEY WANT IT TO...
BUT I THINK YOU'LL WAKE UP TO SOME VERY GOOD NEWS TOMORROW MORNING.

Chapter Eleven

ONE, TWO, THREE, FOUR...
FIVE, SIX, SEVEN, EIGHT...
BAAA...BY!
BAA!
BAABY! BAABY! BAABY
BAA!
GO AWAY! I'M ALLERGIC TO YOU!
SNIFF SNIFF

WHAT'S THAT?
SNIFF SNIFF
SNIFF SNIFF
SNIFF! SNIFF!
SNIFF! SNIFF!
NOAH + LIAM'S ROOM

CREAK!
OH!
SOB
SNIFF SNIFF

WHAT'S WRONG?
I MISS MOMMY AND DADDY!
SHHH! DON'T WAKE UP NOAH.
SOB SOB
DO YOU WANT ME TO GET GRANDMA?
NOOO! DON'T LEAVE ME!!!
SQUEEZE
OKAY...WILL YOU BE QUIET AND GO TO SLEEP IF I STAY FOR A LITTLE BIT?
NOD NOD

CREEEAK

DON'T LEAVE ME!!
I'LL BE RIGHT BACK —
DON'T GO!
I'LL STAY IF YOU'RE QUIET.
ZIP
THERE! HAPPY?
ZZZIP

MAGGIE?
UH-HUH?
HOW COME YOU DON'T LIKE ME AND NOAH?
WHAT? I...
'CAUSE YOU TOLD MOM AND DAD ABOUT MY MICE!! THAT'S WHY!
I KNOW, BUT BEFORE THAT...YOU DIDN'T LIKE US BEFORE, TOO. HOW COME?
I DON'T **NOT** LIKE YOU. YOU JUST DON'T NEED ME. YOU'VE GOT NOAH. YOU GUYS HAVE ALWAYS HAD EACH OTHER.

OH...WELL, CAN I TELL YOU A SECRET?
WHAT?
SOMETIMES NOAH CAN BE KINDA... OVERWHELMING.
DON'T TELL HIM I SAID THAT, THOUGH. PROMISE?
HAH
PROMISE.
MAGGIE?
WHAT?

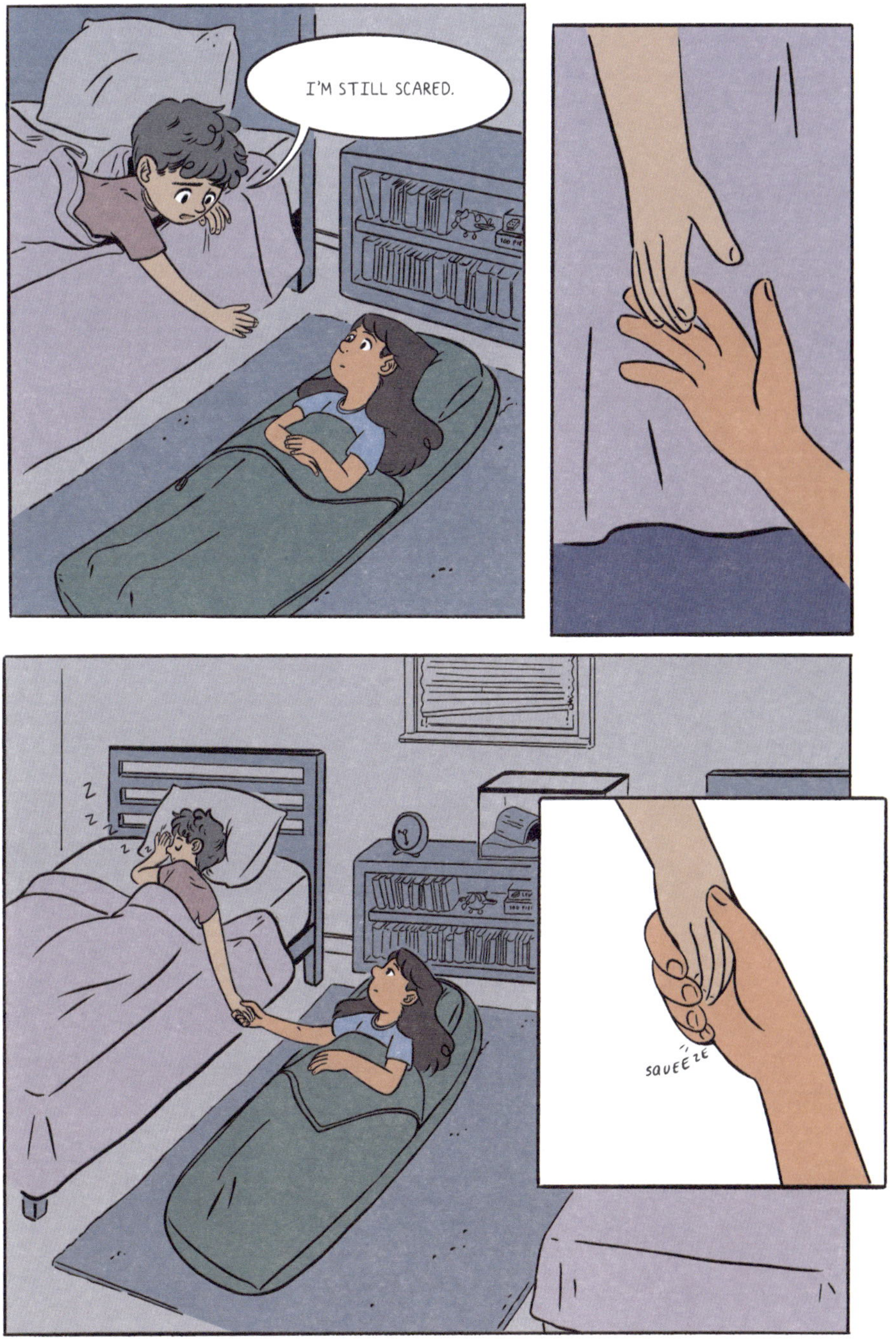
I'M STILL SCARED.
Z
Z
Z
Z
SQUEEZE

THE NEXT MORNING
TIP TOE TIPTOE
GOOD MORNING! AND CONGRATULATIONS. YOU HAVE A NEW LITTLE SISTER!

A SISTER?!
BORN AT ELEVEN O'CLOCK ON THE DOT. WANT TO SEE A PICTURE?
SLIDE
PHEW!
NO NAME YET, SO WE'D BETTER GET BRAINSTORMING.
CAN WE GO SEE MOM AND DAD?
WE'LL GO IN A FEW HOURS. YOUR MOM AND THE BABY HAVE SOME SLEEP TO CATCH UP ON FIRST.

IT'S A GIRL!
SHE LOOKS LIKE AN OLD LADY!
YEAH — LIKE YOU, GRANDMA!
SHE IS RATHER BEAUTIFUL.
I'M HUNGRY!

WELL, WE'VE GOT CEREAL. OR FREEZER WAFFLES.
I WISH DADDY WAS HERE. HE ALWAYS MAKES GOOD BREAKFASTS.
HAPPY BIRTHDAY! READY FOR SOME PANCAKES?
MAYBE WE CAN MAKE PANCAKES...TOGETHER? THEY COULD BE BIRTHDAY PANCAKES, SINCE IT'S THE BABY'S BIRTHDAY!

I DID IT!
FLIP
MY TURN NOW!
GOOD JOB!

DING-DONG!
I'LL GET THAT.
OPEN WIDE!
SHAKE
SHWWWP
SHWWWP
MAGGIE, YOUR FRIEND IS HERE!

UH...
UM...
I'M SORRY ABOUT THE MICE. I DIDN'T KNOW YOU'D BE SO ALLERGIC.
IT'S OKAY. WE GOT THEM TOGETHER.
I KNOW, BUT IT WAS MY IDEA.
YEAH, BUT THAT DOESN'T MAKE IT ALL YOUR FAULT...I'M SORRY I GOT SO MAD.
FRIENDS?
FRIENDS.

WE COULD NAME THE BABY...PANCAKE.
OR GRANDMA JUNIOR!
OR WHIPPED CREAM!

HA HA HA HA HA HA HA

I CAN'T BELIEVE YOUR MOM HAD THE BABY! I'VE ALWAYS WANTED A LITTLE BROTHER OR SISTER. AND NOW YOU HAVE THREE. YOU'RE SO LUCKY!
I AM LUCKY...
LUCKY TO HAVE A FRIEND LIKE YOU!
OH!

I'LL BE RIGHT BACK!
I LOVE IT!
BF
F
OH NO, YOURS IS BROKEN.
BF
F
I BET WE CAN FIX IT.

Chapter Twelve

DIRECTORY
Radiology - FLOOR 3
Maternity Ward - FLOOR 2

BA-BUMP
BA-BUMP
BA-BUMP
BA-BUMP
DING
BA-BUMP
BA-BUMP
BA-BUMP

WHAT IF I REALLY AM ALLERGIC TO SOME HUMANS...
LIKE, ONE HUMAN IN PARTICULAR?
COME ALONG, MAGGIE DEAR!

WHAT ROOM IS IT?
NUMBER 304.
LET'S GO!
REMEMBER TO WALK!
304

IN...
PUSH
AND OUT...

CAREFUL, YOU TWO!
HOW'S MY FAVORITE MAGGIE TODAY?
SWOOP
WHY DON'T YOU GO WASH YOUR HANDS SO YOU CAN HOLD HER?
HOLD HER?! WHAT IF I BREAK HER?

I WANNA HOLD HER!
I WANNA HOLD HER, TOO!
I ALREADY TOLD MAGGIE SHE COULD HAVE THE FIRST TURN.
I MISSED YOU!
I MISSED YOU TOO, SWEETIE.
GO AHEAD AND WASH UP, MAGGIE!
YOU SHOULD HAVE HAD TRIPLETS! THEN WE COULD ALL HOLD THEM AT THE SAME TIME!
YEAH!
AND YOU BOYS HAVE TO WASH YOUR HANDS FIRST, TOO.

WANT ME TO GET HER CALMED DOWN FIRST?
WAH
WAH
WAH
WAH
WAH
SHAKE
I JUST WANT TO GET THIS OVER WITH.
PLEASE STOP...
WAA!
WAA!
WAA!

WAA! WAA! WAA!
WAA!
WAAA!
THERE YOU GO. GOOD LITTLE PIPSQUEAK.
HI THERE...BABY. GOOD LITTLE BABY.
WAA!

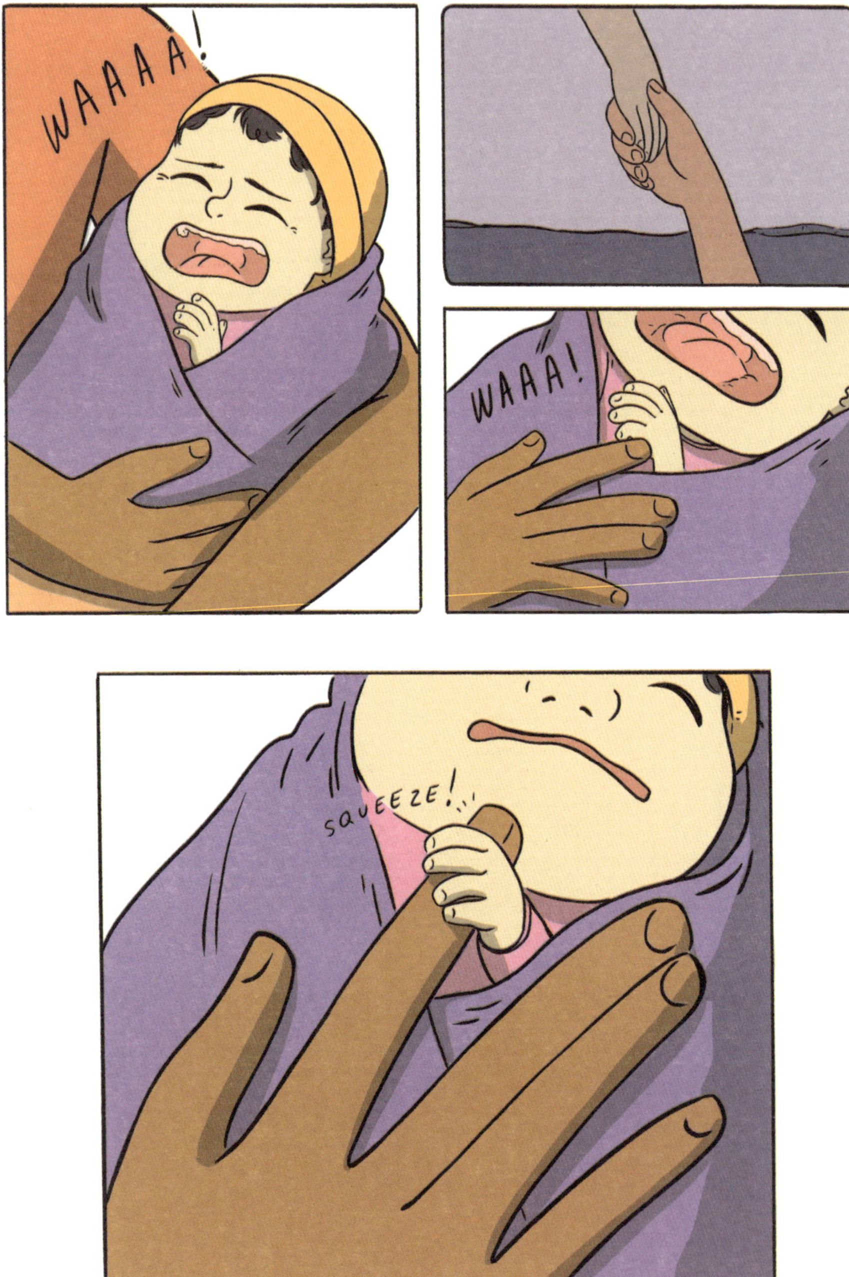
WAAAA!
WAAA!
SQUEEZE!

OH, YOU'RE THE BEST LITTLE BABY IN THE WHOLE WORLD, OH YES YOU ARE!

AWW!
AWWWW!
I THINK WE SHOULD NAME HER JUNE!
HUH...JUNE.
JUNE. YOU KNOW...I THINK I LOVE IT.

Chapter Thirteen

December

January

February

March

April

DON'T YOU WORRY, LITTLE JUNE! SEBASTIAN'S A FOOD-ALLERGY EXPERT.
NO SIGN OF ANY ALLERGIES SO FAR...GOOD AIM, THOUGH.
SPLAT

May

YOU GOT THIS!

June

TA-DA!
HA HA HA
TA-DA!

SCUTTLE
SCUTTLE
CAN WE GO TO THE AQUARIUM TOMORROW?
I DON'T WANNA GO TO THE AQUARIUM.
YEAH. LET'S COME BACK TO THE BEACH AGAIN.
I'M FINE COMING BACK HERE TOMORROW. GET SOME MORE OF THEIR ENERGY OUT...
OKAY. MAGGIE, JUNE, AND I WILL GO TO THE AQUARIUM.

THEY'RE SO SMOOTH!
LIKE SILK.
I'M GLAD I'M NOT ALLERGIC TO THEM.
ME, TOO.
GIGGLE
HA HA HA

I THINK THEY'RE COOL! SO DOES JUNE.
SEE?
COO!

THEY'RE ADORABLE!

I'M SO GLAD WE CAME HERE... YOU'RE JUST FULL OF GREAT IDEAS, MAGGIE.
THANKS, MOM.

MOM?
MM-HMM?
WHAT KIND OF SCIENTIST STUDIES OCEAN ANIMALS?

A MARINE BIOLOGIST.

THAT'S WHAT I'M GONNA BE WHEN I GROW UP. A MARINE BIOLOGIST!

MAAA-GGIE!

Acknowledgments

Thank you to: Ammi-Joan Paquette, for support and enthusiasm from the start. Michelle Mee Nutter, for teaming up, and for incredible, impeccable art. Cassandra Pelham Fulton, for believing in our duo, and for stellar guidance every step of the way. The entire dedicated and creative Scholastic/Graphix team.

Maria Gianferrari and Courtney Pippin-Mathur, for writing lunches and chats. Zara González Hoang, for writing walks and talks. Stacey Donoghue, for helpful early feedback. Anna, the best surprise of my little-kid life. Seth, for never-ending optimism and kindness. And my kids, for believing in *Allergic* from the beginning.

Megan

Thank you to: Megan, for writing such a wonderful story. I couldn't have asked for a better teammate. Kelly Sonnack, for being in my corner as my agent. Ammi-Joan Paquette, for introducing me to *Allergic*. David Saylor and Cassandra Pelham Fulton, for taking a chance on my work. Phil Falco and the whole Graphix team. My amazing flatters, Madison Coyne and Veda Kasireddy.

Mum, Dad, and Joe. Ethan, I love to the moon and back. Thank you for being the reader that inspires me to keep drawing. Greg, for being an amazing partner. Abby, Ryan, Aidan, and Laura. I would truly be lost without all the movie nights, D&D sessions, and hours lying on the floor talking about Ikea furniture.

Finally, thank you for telling me to be open to the possibilities and always reminding me that I could do this. You know who you are, and I will hold that dear to my heart always.

Michelle